TABLE OF CONTENTS

PLOT OVERVIEW

Montana 1948 is set in a small town on the very northeastern edge of the state of Montana. The events described are experienced through the eyes of David Hayden, a twelve-year-old boy. In a prologue, he describes several images he remembers vividly from forty years ago. Years later, after both of his parents are dead, David decides to tell the whole story of the tragedy he witnessed as a boy.

At the time of David's narrative, he lives with his parents in the small town of Bentrock, Montana (population of about 2,000). His father is the county sheriff. His mother also works, as a secretary, so David's parents have hired a local Native American woman as a combination housekeeper and babysitter for their son.

This woman, Marie Little Soldier, falls ill, and David's father summons his brother Frank, who is a doctor. Marie objects to having the doctor examine her but David's father insists on it. After the doctor's visit, Marie tells David's mother why she refused to see him: the doctor has been sexually abusing Native American girls, and Marie was afraid to be alone with him.

David's mother passes on the information to her husband and urges him to take action against his brother for his crimes. David's father begins to investigate and gathers evidence that confirms Marie's accusations.

A few days later, Marie dies. David has seen his Uncle walking from the house and suspects foul play. Len, the deputy sheriff, who lives next door, is also a witness to Frank's presence at the house when Marie died.

David's Uncle Frank has, in fact, murdered the young woman to keep her quiet. David's father takes his brother into custody and locks him in the basement of his own home to avoid scandal.

This makes David's grandfather, a powerful local rancher and former sheriff, furious and he sends four of his hired hands to bust Frank out. David's mother fires a shotgun to keep the cowboys away, and the deputy sheriff hears the shot and comes to defend David and his mother.

On the day David's father has chosen to move his brother to the town jail and to start formal legal proceedings against him, his brother commits suicide.

David's grandfather is furious and severs ties with his surviving son. David and his family move out of state to escape the scandal and family bitterness.

Prologue

Prologue Summary

The prologue describes the narrator's memories of the summer he was twelve years old. These take the form of a series of images, including a very sick young Sioux woman, his father on his knees begging his mother to help him, and his mother loading a shotgun and preparing to use it. He also mentions the sound of breaking glass and the smell of rotting vegetables.

All of these memories are mixed together in David's mind without a clear chronology: "Imagine instead a movie screen divided into boxes or panels, each with its own scene, so that one moment can occur simultaneously with another, . . . so nothing happens before or after, only during" (Prologue, xvi).

Prologue Analysis

The prologue establishes David as the first-person narrator of the book. He points out that he is telling us what happened forty years earlier and that he is the last surviving eyewitness. Now that both of his parents are dead, David feels able to tell the truth about what he knows.

He also establishes the recurring images that he associates with the terrible events. The strongest memories are of sounds, including a woman's coughing, his father's pleading voice asking for help from his mother, the sound of a shotgun blast, and the sound of breaking glass.

David is aware that this crisis led to the revelation of his father's apparent weakness and his mother's strength. David is also a witness to his father's transformation in his role as the sheriff: David's father gets stronger and stronger as he comes to believe in his brother's guilt and insists that Frank is held accountable for his crimes.

The reader is easily convinced, through David's detailed account, that his memories are accurate and that he will be a reliable narrator for the story as it enfolds.

Chapter 1

Chapter 1 Summary

Chapter One begins with David's description of the town of Bentrock, his family, and his life. The town is small and composed primarily of farmers and ranchers and such small business and local government officials as one would expect in a rural county seat.

David's father Wesley Hayden has a special role as sheriff, an office that he inherited from his powerful father. David's mother Gail would much prefer that David's father practice law and live elsewhere, so as not to be dominated by David's grandfather and his family.

There is actually not much for a county sheriff to do in Mercer County, Montana. Life is so hard for the farmers and ranchers in the desolate northern plains that "so much of your attention and energy went into keeping not only yourself but also your family, your crops, and your cattle alive, that nothing was left over for raising hell or making trouble" (Chapter 1, p. 4).

David is disappointed that his father does not fit the typical image of a western sheriff. His father wears a shirt and tie just like a small businessman. Sheriff Hayden does not wear cowboy boots or a Stetson hat or carry a gun. The gun he does have is a small .32 caliber pistol that he keeps in a dresser drawer.

David's impression of his mother is based on her relationship with his father and her attitudes about his own life and future. Gail knows that Wesley, a trained and licensed lawyer, cannot be his true self as long as he follows in his father's footsteps in the small town. She wants her husband to get out of his father's shadow, to move away, and to take up a career as an attorney.

David's mother is concerned about David growing up to be wild. She thinks he is too interested in the landscape and activities such as fishing and hunting that are readily available just outside of town. She wants him to be more civilized than is likely as long as they live in rural Montana.

When the housekeeper/babysitter Marie Little Soldier gets sick with a fever and a serious cough, David's mother is very concerned and she encourages her husband to call his brother, Frank, the doctor.

Marie insists that she does not need a doctor, and Wesley attributes her resistance to Native American superstition. Marie asks David to intervene and keep Dr. Hayden away from her, but David cannot persuade his parents that Marie is right.

Dr. Hayden comes to examine Marie, who insists that Gail be in the room with her while the doctor is present. After Dr. Hayden leaves, Marie tells Gail in private why she didn't want the doctor near her.

David eavesdrops on his parents as Gail tells her husband what Marie has confided to her: that Dr. Hayden has been sexually molesting and raping Native American girls.

Gail wants her husband to do something about Dr. Hayden's crimes. Wesley doesn't want to get involved since Dr. Hayden is his brother. He does, however, agree to hear Marie's accusations.

After their closed-door conversation, David sees his parents emerge "grim-faced and silent." David begins to understand that his Uncle Frank is not who he thought he was. Uncle Frank is, in fact, someone who has hurt people and broken the law.

David's parents conduct an informal investigation by speaking to their next-door neighbors, Len McAuley, the deputy sheriff, and his wife Daisy. Len does not reveal anything, but David overhears Daisy tell Gail that it is known around town that Dr. Hayden "doesn't do everything on the up-and-up." Daisy qualifies her statement with "Just the squaws though."

Gail and David know that Uncle Frank is guilty. David feels that his father knows that his brother is guilty, too. But Sheriff Hayden doesn't want a scandal in town, and he doesn't want to upset his parents.

Chapter 1 Analysis

In the first chapter, the author has David set the stage by describing the novel's rural setting in northeastern Montana. The fictional town of Bentrock is a small community of farmers, ranchers and county workers. The Haydens, David's family, are the most powerful people in town due to David's grandfather's position. Julian Hayden is a rich rancher who has also served several terms as the elected sheriff of the county. His son Wesley, a law school graduate, has taken over the office of sheriff from his father.

David establishes the family dynamic and tensions that exists in his own home. David's father acts as sheriff according to his father's wishes. David's mother Gail wants her husband to leave the town and away from the influence of his dominating father. She wants him to practice law as he was trained to do.

David himself sees his father as somehow ill-suited to the job of sheriff in a Western town. His father does not dress or act the part. For example, he never carries a gun.

David's life is much as might be expected for a boy in rural town. He rides horseback, fishes, and hunts, spending as much time as possible outside and away from the civilizing influences of town and school.

He has a crush on the family's housekeeper and babysitter, Marie Little Soldier. Marie is a strong, young, and lively Native American woman.

The plot begins when Marie gets sick with a serious cough. David's parents call in a local doctor who is David's Uncle Frank. This is the first instance where the reader is made aware of the theme of racism in the novel. Marie expresses fear and resistance to being seen by the doctor, which David's father puts down to Native superstition.

His attitude towards Native Americans means that Sheriff Hayden is disinclined to believe Marie when she accuses Frank of sexually molesting Native girls, however, his wife convinces him that the charges are true and serious.

This event highlights the differences between David's parents and different forms of morality: Wesley is more inclined to act out of loyalty to family or race, while Gail is more morally driven by traditional Christian values. However, David's father does take the law seriously, and once he begins investigating he comes to believe Marie and to realize that he will have to act against his brother Frank.

Chapter 2

Chapter 2 Summary

Sheriff Hayden goes out to the Native American reservation to gather evidence to support Marie's accusations against Dr. Hayden. David also sees the Sheriff consulting with Ollie Young Bear, a respected local Native elder.

That evening, David's father questions Marie again, while David and his mother wait outside. David's mother tells her son how she has never gotten used to Montana and how she longs for the flatlands of her native North Dakota.

The following Sunday, David and his parents have dinner with David's grandparents, Julian and Enid Hayden on their ranch. Wesley talks to his father, and his father mentions that Frank has been involved with Indian girls all his life: "You know Frank's always been partial to red meat. He couldn't have been any older than Davy when Bud caught him down in the stable with that little Indian girl" (Chapter 2, p. 63).

David interrupts the narrative to relate a story about Uncle Frank's bachelor party before he married his wife Gloria. One of Frank's college friends teased Grandfather Hayden about being a hick with cow dung on his boots. The elder Hayden threatened the loudmouth with a gun, and Frank's friend ran away, eliciting great laughter from the Hayden brothers.

After dinner David goes out horseback riding. His grandfather had given him a .22 target pistol, and he enjoys firing many rounds with the new firearm. Before he returns to the ranch house, David shoots a magpie. "I needed that, I thought; I hadn't even known it but I had to kill something. The events, the discoveries, the secrets of the past few days—Marie's illness, Uncle Frank's sins, the tension between my father and mother—had excited something in me that wasn't released until I shot a magpie out of a pinon tree" (Chapter 2, p. 72).

David sees his father and his uncle talking outside and assumes that his Sheriff father is confronting Uncle Frank about his crimes. However, David sees the two brothers shaking hands.

David's father tells his mother that the problem has been solved because Frank has agreed to stop molesting Indian girls. David's mother responds, "That's not the way it works. You know that. Sins—crimes—are not supposed to go unpunished" (Chapter 2, p. 76).

That day, David sees Marie one last time before he goes to sleep; the next day he comes home after fishing with a friend to find Marie dead and the undertaker's hearse at their house. Uncle Frank insists that Marie died of pneumonia, although both David's mother and their neighbor Daisy McAuley believe Marie was getting better.

David is sent next door while Daisy and his mother commiserate. He finds Len, a recovering alcoholic, drinking whiskey. Len tells David, "'you know what your granddad said it means to be a peace officer in Montana? He said it means knowing when to look and when to look away'" (Chapter 2, p. 84).

Later, when David's father returns home after breaking the news of Marie's death to her mother, David tells his father that he saw Uncle Frank leaving their house that afternoon. David also reveals that he thinks Len saw Frank too.

David has trouble sleeping that night as he has a "strange half-dreaming, half-waking vision" of the local Native Americans mourning Marie and perhaps planning to take revenge.

Chapter 2 Analysis

In Chapter Two, the situation becomes more and more serious. Marie dies, and David and most probably Len, the deputy sheriff who lives next door, saw Frank coming from the house at the time of her death. David's father is torn between his loyalty to his brother and his family and his dedication to the law.
Chapter Two also develops the theme of racism through David's grandfather's attitude and statements regarding Native Americans. While Frank's history of sexual relationships with Native American women lends support to Marie's accusations against him, his father's use of the term "red meat" (Chapter 2, p. 63) to describe Native women also points to the that Native women are perceived as and treated like animals. Frank uses Native women to satisfy his sexual appetite, just like he would use meat to satisfy hunger.

Chapter 3

Chapter 3 Summary

Marie's funeral takes place out of state in North Dakota, and the family sends flowers rather than attend the service. However, Sheriff Hayden plunges with renewed energy into investigating Marie's accusations against Frank.

Three days later, Sheriff Hayden arrests Frank and locks him in the basement of his home. He tells his wife that Frank didn't want the public scandal of being put into the county jail, and his brother agreed to put him in the house quietly. Gail Hayden is not happy with the arrangement: "You've turned my laundry room into a *jail!*" (Chapter 3, p. 103).

Sheriff Hayden leaves to inform Frank's wife, Gloria, of his arrest. When he returns, he takes David outside for a private talk. At first, he avoids the real subject at hand, but eventually he asks David to watch out for trouble and to get Len to help if anything happens.

That night Julian and Enid Hayden arrive at Sheriff Hayden's house. Wesley's father is furious at him for arresting his brother and accuses him of doing it out of jealousy. Sheriff Hayden is forced to tell his father that his brother has committed sexual assault. Julian Hayden dismisses this accusation because the victims were only Native Americans. Sheriff Hayden finally tells his father that Frank is suspected of murder.

David is surprised and frightened when his father stands up to his powerful grandfather, who says threateningly, "My God. My God, boy. Stop this before I have to." However, Sheriff Hayden knows he is doing the right thing: "This isn't for any of us to stop or start. This has to go its own way" (Chapter 3, p. 114).

David has been listening through a heating grate. He comes downstairs to see his father on his knees seeking comfort from his mother "Help me with this Gail" (Chapter 3, p. 115).

The next day, David's grandfather sends four of his cowboys to bust Frank out of Wesley's basement. David searches frantically for his father and Len but cannot find them. His mother loads the shotgun they keep in the house and fires a warning shot at the intruders. At the sound of the shot, Len comes to the rescue and forces the men away at gunpoint.

David's father says he will call his father and get him to stop trying to rescue Frank. However, David's mother has had enough; she just wants Frank out of her home so she can feel safe again.

Sheriff Hayden agrees to release Frank and goes down into the basement. However, he returns alone. "He's guilty as sin, Gail. He told me as much. . . . Maybe a jury will cut him loose. I won't. *By God, I won't.*"

During the night Frank starts breaking all of the glass canning jars in the root cellar. The sound of this destruction heightens David's family's anxiety.

In the morning, Sheriff Hayden prepares to take Frank to the county jail. He goes down to the basement with two cups of coffee. David hears his father cry out "*Oh, no. Oh my God, no!*" (Chapter 3, p. 153). David goes down the steps to find his uncle in a pool of blood. Uncle Frank has committed suicide by slashing his wrists.

David has mixed feelings about his Uncle's death, but the overriding emotion is relief that the scandal, tension and danger are over. "I felt something for my uncle in death that I hadn't felt for him in life. It was gratitude, yes, but it was something more. It was very close to love" (Chapter 3, p. 156).

Chapter 3 Analysis

Chapter Three includes two events significant to the development of the plot. In the first, David's grandfather sends four cowhands to the house to break Frank out of confinement. In the face of this threat, David's mother loads a shotgun, although she has never fired such a weapon before. She is willing to resort to violence to defend her home and herself and her son.

When David's father arrives, the men are gone and the immediate threat is over. However, David's mother is frightened and exhausted. She insists that her husband get the prisoner out of their home, even if it means releasing a criminal. This is a major shift for her character who up until this point has insisted that Frank be held accountable for his crimes.

David's father agrees to release Uncle Frank to avoid further endangering his home and family. However, when he talks to Frank he changes his mind. Frank has admitted his guilt and shown no remorse. Frank is a racist who believes killing a

Native American is not a crime. Both Gail and Wesley undergo a significant change in attitude in this chapter. Gail had previously demanded that Frank should pay the price for his crimes but is willing to let him go to ensure the safety of her family. Wesley, on the other hand, has been reluctant to enforce the law where his brother is concerned until he realizes that Frank is not only guilty but he feels no remorse. Confronted with this fact, Wesley chooses legal justice over his family loyalty.

The second major event in Chapter Three occurs the next morning. When David's father goes into the basement to take Frank to jail, he finds that his brother has committed suicide. This reinforces the idea that the Hayden family live by their own rules; Frank would rather take his own life than face the consequences of his actions like an ordinary person.

David's father is crushed by the loss of his brother. Surprisingly, however, David is relieved and grateful that the family's problems have been solved raising questions about where he stands on the moral scale the novel has established.

Epilogue

Epilogue Summary

At Uncle Frank's funeral, David notices the split in the family with Frank's wife Gloria and his grandparents on one side of the grave while he and his parents stand on the other.

The whole family agrees not to reveal Frank's crimes but, instead, to say that he died in an accident, falling off a ladder in the basement. Frank is eulogized as a war hero and a solid citizen.

David's mother grows increasingly uncomfortable with living a lie, and she asks her husband to leave the town and start over elsewhere. David's father agrees, and they move to Fargo, North Dakota, near Mrs. Hayden's parents. David's father joins a local law firm and becomes a partner.

Meanwhile, Len has been elected sheriff but is unable to serve out his term because of a disabling stroke. David's grandfather also has a stroke, and he does not survive. David wonders if the strain of keeping secrets contributed to the two men's brains breaking down. He also notes that his father's bitterness may well have contributed to the cancer that eventually killed him.

David becomes a history teacher in Minnesota. But he is a skeptic about what history books call the truth. He knows that many important events can and will be kept secret, as was the case in his own family history.

The book ends with David's wife commenting to her in-laws about the family history: "David told me about what happened when you lived in Montana. That sure was the Wild West, wasn't it?"

David's father responds loudly: "Don't blame Montana. Don't ever blame Montana!" (Epilogue p.169).

Epilogue Analysis

The Epilogue covers the fallout from Uncle Frank's suicide. It describes how the family agreed to lie about Frank's death saying that he died accidentally, by falling off a ladder in the basement. This decision effectively covers over Frank's crimes and undoes Wesley's decision to bring his brother to justice.

Not surprisingly, Frank's wife Gloria and David's grandparents blame Sheriff Hayden for his death. This is symbolized when the two sides of the family stand on opposite sides of Frank's grave at the burial.

Soon the tension and stress become too much for David's mother and the family move to Fargo in North Dakota. . David's father becomes a successful lawyer in their new town. This raises the questions of whether David's mother was right all along; was her husband was wrong to go back to Montana after law school and spend his life under his father's influence?

David's father has had to learn several lessons the hard way. Racism, even in its mildest form, leads to negative and often tragic outcomes. Family loyalty must give way to the law, which, in most cases, is designed to the whole community, rather than just some powerful individuals.

The story is written as a coming-of-age narrative, chronicling David's loss of innocence. He has observed the impact of sexual assault and murder and seen power at work in a community that hides secrets. David is certainly changed by the events he recounts and his decision to become a history teacher suggests that he continues to be interested in the ways that the past continues to affect the present and the way in which certain events get left out of the official story of the past. His skepticism about the truthfulness of history reflects the lessons he learned in the aftermath of his Uncle's death when the Haydens conspired to cover up Frank's crimes. In doing so they also covered up the fact that racism was still prevalent in their community and silenced the Native women that Frank abused and, in Marie's case, killed.

MAJOR CHARACTER ANALYSIS

David Hayden

David is the author of the story and the first-person narrator of the book. He writes the story forty years after the events, once everyone else, especially his parents and grandparents, are dead. The tale he records involves accusations of sexual abuse against his father's brother, David's Uncle Frank. David at the time was 12 years old. He was still considered a child by his family, and he gathered information by eavesdropping on adults.

In the story, the young adolescent David is intelligent, curious, sensitive, loving, and energetic. In many ways, he is what the reader would expect of a 12-year-old boy. He has a crush on his housekeeper/babysitter, Marie.

David still pursues his boyhood activities, such as horseback riding and fishing. However, he is very eager to be a full member of the family and to be treated like an adult. David is very fond of his mother and father and feels loved and taken care of.

David's life changes with the revelations of his Uncle's crimes and the murder and suicide that follow. As David looks back on events as an adult, he recognizes that they contributed to his skepticism about life and history, which he teaches. He knows first-hand about the hidden secrets that are not included in history textbooks.

Wesley Hayden

Wesley is David's father, the sheriff in the town of Bentrock, Montana. Sheriff Hayden is intelligent and well educated; he has graduated from law school and passed the bar exam. He is 38 years old at the time of the story.

He has become the sheriff because his father was sheriff before him and persuaded him to follow in his footsteps. In David's eyes, his father is not suited to his job. He is not a controlling or dominating figure like his grandfather. Wesley Hayden does not believe in violence and does not carry a gun.

David's father also suffers in comparison to his older brother, Frank. Frank is a war hero from World War II and a successful doctor in the town. Frank was also a star athlete. Wesley was injured as a youngster so he was not athletic and was 4F during the war.

Sheriff Hayden is prejudiced against Native Americans. He and David are the two characters who change most in the novel. Sheriff Hayden, in particular, comes to believe in equality before the law for Native and white people in the end. He suffers greatly to learn this lesson.

Wesley Hayden's racism is his tragic flaw and initiates the chain of events that result in two deaths and the destruction of a family. If he had treated Marie as an equal and honored her request to keep Dr. Hayden away from her, Marie would not have accused Frank Hayden of sexual assault. Since Wesley treats Marie as a superstitious child, the truth comes to light.

Wesley Hayden eventually dies of cancer, which David attributes to his bitterness about being rejected by his family after his brother, Frank's death. David's father's early death is also a kind of karmic justice for all the harm that arose out of his racist attitudes.

Gail Hayden

Originally a farm girl from North Dakota, Gail is David's mother. She works as a secretary and is intelligent, loving, principled, and strong.   She is, generally, calm and competent in a crisis.

Mrs. Hayden disagrees with her husband's choice to stay in his hometown and follow his father's wishes by becoming sheriff. She would much prefer that the family live elsewhere and that her husband practice as a lawyer.

Mrs. Hayden's being a woman is very important, because she immediately believes Marie's accusations against Dr. Hayden. This suggests that women are more aware of and concerned about the reality of sexual violence. It is also important that Mrs. Hayden is Christian and has a strong sense of right and wrong, as this allows her to be the voice of morality for much of the novel.

In the climax of the novel, Mrs. Hayden proves her strength when she defends herself and David from intruders with a shotgun.

Dr. Frank Hayden

Frank is charming, handsome, athletic, and charismatic. He is also racist, self-indulgent, abusive, violent, and narcissistic.

David's Uncle Frank has always been the golden boy of the family, David's grandfather's favorite. This has led to his sense of entitlement and being above the law. He indulges his sexual desires by abusing Native American girls and gets away with it for a long time.

When his brother Wesley confronts him about his crimes, Frank reveals his deep prejudice against Native Americans. After he murders Marie, his accuser, he expresses no remorse because she was only a Native.

Dr. Hayden does, however, have a sense of shame. When he is threatened with a public trial and scandal, he chooses suicide instead of facing humiliation.
Marie Little Soldier

Marie is a young, vital, strong Native American woman who cares for David after school and does housekeeping for the family while David's mother works.

In his early adolescence, David finds Marie sexy and attractive. David feels very close to Marie and is heartbroken when she is killed.

Marie's illness is the catalyst for the whole plot. When the family summons Dr. Hayden, she objects to letting him examine her. Then she tells Mrs. Hayden about Frank's reputation for sexually assaulting Native American girls, and the tragic events begin to unfold.

Julian Hayden

Julian is David's grandfather, a rich and powerful rancher and former sheriff. He is proud, strong, dominating, violent, and racist. He does care for his family, especially for his favorite son Frank and his grandson David.

Unlike David's father, David's grandfather does carry a gun and uses it as a threat. Julian is deeply prejudiced against Native Americans, referring to Frank's conquests as "red meat."

Julian is also averse to scandal and helps to cover up the truth about Frank's death. He dies of a stroke, which David attributes to the strain of keeping Frank's crimes and suicide a secret.

Len McAuley

Len is Wesley Hayden's deputy and was deputy for Julian Hayden before that. Len is a crucial witness: he sees Frank leaving the sheriff's house after Frank has murdered Marie.

He proves to be heroic in two major ways: he has the integrity to stand up to David's grandfather when Julian asks him to help get Frank out of confinement. He also rescues David and his mother when Julian sends four cowboys to free Frank by force.

THEMES

Racism

The prejudice of white people towards Native Americans is the primary theme of *Montana 1948*.

David is very much aware of his father's garden-variety racism; it came up when he forbade his son to wear a pair of moccasins: "He wears those and soon he'll be as flat-footed and lazy as an Indian." To David's father, all Native Americans are assumed to be lesser citizens. They are by race lazy, irresponsible, and guided by primitive superstitions.

When the Haydens' housekeeper, Marie, objects to being examined by David's uncle, who is a local doctor, David's father assumes that Marie is reacting out of superstition and resistance to modern medicine. Later Marie shares her true motivation with David's mother: Uncle Frank has a history of sexually abusing Native American women.

All of the men in the Hayden family, David's father, grandfather, and uncle, are explicitly racist in the novel. David's grandfather refers to Native American women as "red meat." Uncle Frank believes he can get away with sexual assault because no one really cares what happens to Native women and girls.

David himself has a crush on Marie, and he feels most free and happy when playing with Marie and her boyfriend. He seems to be free of the racist attitudes of his family and society, perhaps as a result of having Marie, a vital, caring Native American woman, in his life as a child.

Coming of Age/Adolescence

David writes the narrative from his perspective forty years after the event. It is, however, essential that he was 12 years old at the time, transitioning from childhood into adolescence. David often thinks about how his parents and others still treated him as a child who needed protection from serious and frightful adult problems.

He gathers information on Uncle Frank's crimes and his father's investigation by eavesdropping. Knowing what is going on but being in a position where he is not supposed to know causes him a great deal of stress.

Eventually, his parents include him to some extent. However, even at the end of the story, David still feels like a child. He specifically thinks that after Uncle Frank's suicide his family life will return to normal. His forty-year-old self chalks this assumption up to childish innocence.

Montana 1948 is a coming-of-age story. It begins with an innocent child who enjoys fishing with his friends and follows him as he learns about the secrets of the adult world. By the end of the novel, David still sees some things from a child's point of view, but he is no longer innocent of grown-up problems. In a matter of a few days he has become a young adult.

Wild West

The setting of *Montana 1948* is clearly the American West. . Mercer County, Montana, is still a place where men carry guns, and the sheriff is the law and the local economy is still based largely on cattle ranching.

David's grandfather is a throwback to the "Wild West", where problems were solved with power and violence. When David's father, the sheriff, locks up his brother Frank, Julian Hayden sends four cowboys with an ax to break Frank out. He considers this an appropriate solution to the problem of his son's arrest. If he has power and muscle on his side, he wins. Julian Hayden is not interested in the niceties of polite and more civilized behavior.

Even David's mother realizes that she is living in the Wild West and occasionally has to act according to its rules. When threatened, she loads her husband's shotgun and fires a warning shot at the intruders. She knows that in the environment she lives in force only recognizes a stronger force.

David himself is also affected by his environment. He relieves his tension about his Uncle Frank by shooting a bird, saying: "I needed to kill something." David is another product of the Wild West attitudes and behaviors that pervade his family and his town.

Law and Law Enforcement

David's father is a lawyer, and his job as sheriff requires him to enforce the law. He has great difficulty reconciling his belief in the legal system and the reality of arresting and prosecuting his own bother. He investigates as he should and determines that Frank is guilty. Yet, at first, he is willing to let his brother off as long as Frank promises to stop his criminal behavior.

Eventually, David's father comes to believe that the law is more important than family loyalty. He realizes that the law treats all people equally, including Native Americans. The Hayden family and the citizens of Bentrock, Montana, are willing to ignore Frank's crimes because of their racist attitudes towards Native American people. David's father recognizes that the law needs to take its course no matter what his family or the community think is tolerable. Frank must receive just punishment for his crimes.

It is significant that David's father goes on to practice law after his brother dies. David, however, has seen how the system favors the rich and powerful—everyone agrees that Frank would have been likely to escape serious punishment from a friendly jury. David cannot see himself as a lawyer within such a system, and he becomes a teacher instead.

Family Loyalty

Montana 1948 can be described as an extended examination of the conflict between morality and family loyalty.

At first, David's parents are on opposite sides. David's mother wants Frank to be punished. David's father wants to keep his family happy and avoid scandal.

David witnesses the two brothers discussing the accusations and overhears his father saying that Frank will stop his sexual misdeeds. David's mother is not at all satisfied with this outcome. She insists that her husband fulfill his role as enforcer of the law and bring Frank to justice.

By the end of the novel, David's father has come to believe that Frank does in fact deserve to be tried and sentenced for his crimes. His change in attitude results, in part, from Frank's total lack of remorse. Frank feels justified in killing Marie to protect himself because he does not value the life of a Native American. David's father knows that this is not right. Frank is a criminal; it doesn't matter whose son or brother or husband he is.

SYMBOLS AND MOTIFS

Air and Breathing

The first image in the book is the sound of Marie coughing. She is sick and having trouble breathing. She may have pneumonia. Later on she is murdered, perhaps by being smothered by a pillow.

When she feels stressed, David's mother longs for the wind that sweeps across the plains of her native North Dakota. It is the thought of the air and the air in motion that helps her to let go of the tension she is feeling.

The clearest use of the symbols of air and breathing are in relation to David himself: "As I had so often been advised by my parents, I never believed any of my grandmother's supernatural stories. Until the day Marie died. That night I lay in bed and couldn't breathe. The room felt close, full, as though someone else was getting the oxygen I needed" (Chapter 2, p. 87). Marie's death literally takes his breath away.

At the climax of the book, David's mother fires a shotgun, and the shot symbolically changes the atmosphere: "The air seemed instantly altered, turned foul, the stuff of rank, black chemical smoke and not he sweet, clean oxygen we daily breathed" (Chapter 3, p. 130).

The author plays on the reader's expectation that the air in the open spaces of Montana will be clean and clear. When the people who live there face extreme stress, the very air and their breathing patterns change. Their inner struggles are reflected in their breathing the air around them.

Guns and Firearms

The shotgun blast, mentioned above, signals the climax of the novel. Moreover, the symbolism of guns and firearms pervades the whole story.

David considers his father a man too weak to be sheriff, in part because Wesley Hayden does not carry a gun. Sheriff Hayden keeps the small gun he owns in a dresser drawer.

David has another role model when it comes to using firearms. David's grandfather does carry a gun, and even the threat of his using it carries weight.

David himself releases stress by firing his .22 and killing a bird with his firearm.

Len, the deputy sheriff, also carries a gun, a properly large .44 or .45, which he uses to fend off the cowboys sent by Julian Hayden. In this instance, the gun symbolizes strength and is used to protect a woman and child from attack.

Guns and firearms are fully integrated into the culture of the West as depicted in the novel. They can be used both positively and negatively. They are an outlet for all kinds of emotions, including anger, fear, stress, and love.

House and Home

Initially, the novel employs the symbol of the family home in a conventional way. David comes home after school and expects to find the housekeeper Marie at home to care for him until his mother gets home from work.

Marie, however, is ill. Sickness has entered David's normally safe haven. Then the situation gets much, much worse.

Marie is murdered in the house, and David feels the presence of death there. David's father arrests his uncle and locks him in the basement of the house. The Haydens' home has become a jail.

After the cowboys threaten to break into their home, David's mother insists that her husband let his prisoner go so that she can once again feel safe in her home.

After Uncle Frank commits suicide in the basement, the house is further tainted by violent death, and the family sells it and moves away.

Thus, the Haydens' home symbolizes all of the troubles they experience in the novel. They start out safe in their home, and their safe haven is compromised and destroyed during the story.

Town and Wilderness

David sees the town as a civilized environment that limits his freedom. He spends as much time as possible outside the town away from everything that alienates him from community life. In David's mind, the town "stood for social order, good manners, the chimed schedules of school and church. It was a world meant for storekeepers, teachers, ministers, for the rule-makers, the order-givers, the law-enforcers".

David is a growing adolescent: he wants to be free of his parents and free of all influences that tie him down.

In the important sequence when David goes out into the countryside from his grandparents' house, he is at his wildest. He shoots his gun at everything and kills a magpie.

Burial and Graves

When David kills the bird, he makes a point of burying it. He hides what he is ashamed of so others cannot see it.

In a more symbolic way, David's father hides his criminal brother in the basement rather than taking him to jail where everyone in town can see what is happening. His confinement in the basement foreshadows Frank's impending death and burial underground. When Uncle Frank commits suicide, the family hides his body so only the undertaker will see his slashed wrists.

Frank's actual grave represents a chasm in the family with a literal gulf between David and his parents on one side and David's grandparents and Frank's wife on the other side.

David

David is the only character in the novel with a biblical name. By calling his protagonist and narrator David, the author suggests parallels with the ancient character of David.

The biblical David is given credit for writing the Book of Psalms, which, in part, records the history of his people. The narrator David writes the history of his family and his community.

David first appears in the Bible as a young man who fights and slays the giant, Goliath, against all odds. The biblical David came of age on the battlefield. In the novel, David comes of age in the Wild West, where violent death makes life like a battlefield.

IMPORTANT QUOTES

1. "The harshness of the land and the flattening effect of wind and endless sky probably accounted for the relative tranquility of Mercer County. Life was simply too hard, and so much of your attention and energy went into keeping not only yourself but also your family, your crops, and your cattle alive, that nothing was left over for raising hell or making trouble."(Chapter 1, p. 4)

   This is David's interpretation of life in rural Montana. It explains for him why his father, the Sheriff does not deal with the stereotypical problems of the rural West, such as wild cowboys and drunken Native Americans and so on. David's father doesn't even carry a gun on the job.

2. "Why did my grandfather first run for sheriff? ... He wanted, he needed power. He was a dominating man who drew sustenance and strength from controlling others. To him being the law's agent probably seemed a natural progression— first you master the land and its beasts, then you regulate the behavior of men and women."(Chapter 1, pp. 8-9)

   This is a summary of Julian Hayden's character and foreshadows the family conflict in the novel. When David's father goes against his own father's wishes, the elder Hayden reacts. He will even resort to violence against his family when challenged.

3. "The problem was that I wanted to grow up wild. . . . Wildness meant, to me, getting out of town and into the country. Even our small town—really, in 1948, still a frontier town in many respects—tasted to me like pabulum. It stood for social order, good manners, the chimed schedules of school and church. It was a world meant for storekeepers, teachers, ministers, for the rule-makers, the order-givers, the law-enforcers. And in my case, my parents were not only figurative agents of the law, my father *was* the law." (Chapter 1, p. 10)

   This is the not surprising point of view of a twelve-year-old boy on the verge of adolescence and increasingly aware of how his parents controlled his childhood. David wants to be independent, free, and able to make his own choices. He is able to do that when he is outside the town fishing or shooting or horseback riding.

4. "(I realize now how much I was a part of that era's thinking: I never wondered then, as I do now, why a college didn't snap up an athlete like Ronnie. Then, I knew without being told, as if it were knowledge that I drank in with the water, that college was not for Indians)." (Chapter 1, p. 14)

   This is the first introduction of the theme of racism as it applies to all Native Americans in the West. White people assume that Native Americans are second-class citizens who do not deserve a college education or a professional career.

5. "My father did not like Indians. . . . He believed Indians, with only a few exceptions, were ignorant, lazy, superstitious, and irresponsible. I first learned of his racism when I was seven or eight. An aunt gave me a pair of moccasins for my birthday, and my father forbade me to wear them. . . . 'He wears those and soon he'll be as flat-footed and lazy as an Indian.'" (Chapter 1, p. 22)

   David says his father would not have recognized his own prejudices. Sheriff Hayden might well have said that he was just describing reality as he observed it around town and on the reservation. This turns out to be a major area of character development over the course of the book. By the end of the novel, David's father is convinced that the effects of racism, including his brother's murder of a Native American woman, are not to be condoned.

6. "Your brother makes his patients—some of his patients—undress completely and get into indecent positions. . . . He fondles their breasts. He—no you don't turn away. *Don't!* You asked, and I am going to tell you. All of it. He puts things into these girls. Inside them, *there*. His instruments. His fingers. He has … your brother I believe has inserted his, his penis into some of these girls. Wesley, your brother is *raping* these women. These *girls*. These Indian girls." (Chapter 1, p. 36)

   This is the climactic speech of Chapter One. David's mother obviously believes Marie's accusations against Dr. Hayden. David's father remains to be convinced, but the sheriff does move quickly to question Marie himself and start an investigation. The rest of the plot follows inevitably from this moment.

7. "Daisy's usually loud, brassy voice was lowered, but I heard her say, 'The word is he doesn't do everything on the up-and-up.' Then she noticed me. She straightened up and smiled at me but stopped talking. That meant I was

supposed to leave the room, and I did. But slowly. As I crossed into the living room, Daisy whispered, 'Just the squaws though.'" (Chapter 1, p. 40)

David overhears the wife of Len, the deputy sheriff, confirming Marie's accusations against Dr. Hayden. David is also aware that as a "child" he is not supposed to hear this adult conversation.

8. "I wanted to be included, to know more than my eavesdropping brought me. I suppose I wanted adult status, to have my parents discuss the case in front of me, not to . . . have them speak in code as if I were a baby who could be kept in ignorance by grown-ups spelling words in his presence." (Chapter 2, p. 54)

David is very much aware throughout the novel that his parents are still trying to protect their child from the knowledge of evil and crime in their family. David is at an age where he chafes at being treated as a child or a baby. He wants to be a full-fledged grown-up himself.

9. "Had I any sensitivity at all I might have recognized that all this talk about wind and dirt and mountains and childhood was my mother's way of saying she wanted a few moments of purity, a temporary escape from the sordid drama that was playing itself out in her own house. But I was on the trail of something that would lead me out of childhood." (Chapter 2, p. 56)

This quotation suggests David's mother's inner feelings about the investigation into Uncle Frank's crimes. It foreshadows the scene later when David's mother insists that her husband just let Frank go and end the tension and danger.

10. "You know Frank's always been partial to red meat. He couldn't have been any older than Davy when Bud caught him down in the stable with that little Indian girl. Bud said to me, 'Mr. Hayden, you better have a talk with the boy.'. . . I wouldn't be surprised if there wasn't some young ones out on the reservation who look a lot like your brother." (Chapter 2, pp. 62-63)

Here, David's grandfather confirms that Uncle Frank has been sexually involved with Native American girls all his life. Julian Hayden also makes a directly racist statement by referring to Native women as "red meat."

11. "This city fellow thinks he's heard enough. . . . He starts for our table. By the time he gets there Pop has pulled out the little .32 revolver of his. . . . 'Out in Montana you wouldn't be worth dirtying a man's hands on. Or his boots. So we'd handle him this way. Nice and clean.' And he keeps holding the gun on him. . . . Meanwhile Frank's laughing so hard he gets *me* going and then neither one of us can stop." (Chapter 2, p. 56)

    This passage helps to define the character of David's grandfather. He uses threats of violence when provoked. He carries a gun and will use it. The fact that his sons think threatening someone with a gun is funny also says a great deal about their attitudes toward violence.

12. "I needed that, I thought; I hadn't even known it but I had to kill something. The events, the discoveries, the secrets of the past few days—Marie's illness, Uncle Frank's sins, the tension between my father and mother—had excited something in me that wasn't released until I shot a magpie out of a pinon tree." (Chapter 2, p. 72)

    This reveals how intense the situation is for David. He wants to be an adult and participate in real life. Yet he is still emerging from childhood and the stress of the circumstances in his family trouble him greatly. His need to commit a violent act suggests that he shares the violent inclinations of his father, uncle and grandfather. The dead magpie also foreshadows the death of Marie.

13. "'You know what your granddad said it means to be a peace officer in Montana? He said it means knowing when to look and when to look away. Took me a while to learn that.' Len leaned forward and pointed a long, gnarled finger at me. 'Your dad hasn't quite got the hang of it. Not just yet.'" (Chapter 2, p. 84)

    Len, the deputy sheriff, is suggesting that David's father would be better off ignoring his brother's crimes. Some people, like the powerful Haydens, are truly considered above the law.

14. "As I had so often been advised by my parents, I never believed any of my grandmother's supernatural stories. Until the day Marie died. That night I lay in bed and couldn't breathe. The room felt close, full, as though someone else was getting the oxygen I needed." (Chapter 2, p. 87)

This passage uses the symbolism of breathing that begins with Marie's coughing at the very beginning of the book. It also suggests that Uncle Frank may well have killed Marie by suffocating her with a pillow. Thus, Marie's ghost may be trying to tell David something.

15. "'If I had my way, I'd let every house in town go. Let the sun bake 'em and the north wind freeze 'em until there isn't a house in town with a spot of paint on it. You'd see this town from a distance and it would look like nothing but firewood and gray stone. And maybe you'd keep right on moving because it looked like nothing was living here. Paint. Fresh paint. That's how you find life and civilization. Women come and they want fresh paint.'" (Chapter 3, pp. 105-106)

David's father has just locked his brother Frank in his basement. He is exhausted by the tension and conflict he feels between loyalty to his family and faithfulness to the law. He imagines escaping his troubled reality by having the whole town disappear.

16. "It is commonplace to refer to the narrowness and intolerance of small town life, but it seems to me just the opposite was true, at least of Bentrock, Montana, in 1948. The citizens of that community tolerated all kinds of behavior, from the eccentric to the unusual to the aberrant." (Chapter 3, p. 121)

David wonders how it is that people know about his Uncle Frank's molesting his patients and yet keep it secret. The small-town people he knows make a point of avoiding scandal and making trouble. Perhaps they expect the same leeway for themselves and their families.

17. "I began to feel dizzy and ashamed and sick because this time, with Loretta, the thought of how Uncle Frank may have abused her did not disgust me as it had with Miss Schott, but stirred me sexually." (Chapter 3, p. 122)

Twelve-year-old David is entering adolescence and experiencing changing hormones, thoughts, and bodily responses. It is another aspect of his coming-of-age story. His sexual response to the thought of his Uncle abusing a young woman suggests that he shares some of Frank's desires but his shame at his arousal distinguishes him from his Uncle.

18. "I was running back across the street when the shotgun boomed, and its blast was so loud, so wrongly out of place along that quiet, tree-lined, middle-class American street that the air seemed instantly altered, turned foul, the stuff of rank, black chemical smoke and not he sweet, clean oxygen we daily breathed." (Chapter 3, p. 130)

    David's mother's firing the shotgun is shocking. It is something David could never have imagined happening. The imagery of the air suddenly turning foul instead of clean is an apt metaphor for the whole story of Uncle Frank and the affect his crimes have on David's family and the community more generally.

19. "As my father spoke . . . what struck me was that he seemed to be apologizing. For what? I wondered. For not being there when those men came? How could he have known? He was at work, where he was supposed to be. For being Frank Hayden's brother? Julian Hayden's son? Even then I knew that we were not responsible for the circumstances of our birth or the sins of our fathers." (Chapter 3, pp. 135-36)

    By this time David is acutely aware of the "sins of our fathers" as it applies to his grandfather, who raised his sons to be racists and to consider themselves above the law. However, he still considers his own father to be a good and law-abiding man.

20. "So, yes I mean it. Let him go. Let him do whatever he wants to whomever he wants. I don't care anymore. I just want my house back. I want my family safe." (Chapter 3, p. 137)

    David's mother is exhausted and traumatized by the discovery of frank's crimes and the threat from Julian Hayden and his men. She is ready to sacrifice justice for safety. This puts the responsibility on her husband to make a decision. Sheriff Hayden then decides not to release his brother. It is a major turning point in the novel.

21. "I was still child enough to believe, as children do, that when adults are engaged in adult business children become invisible. That was why it was so unsettling to have my father staring at me. What did he want from me? Was he waiting for me to express an opinion—I was the only one in the room who hadn't. Didn't he know—I was a child and ineligible to vote? How dare he bring me in on this

now—I wasn't even supposed to know the facts in the case!" (Chapter 3, p. 139)

This passage sums up the tension David has felt throughout the events of the story. He is both a child who is supposed to be protected from evil and an important part of his family who shares his parents' experiences and emotions. It is an uncomfortable position to be in, and it disturbs David greatly.

22. "'I don't care. I tell you, if you could hear him talk. As if he had no more concern for what he did than if . . . if he had kicked a dog. No. He'd show more remorse over a dog. . . . Do you see?' asked my father. 'I can't let him loose. Not and live with myself.'" (Chapter 3, p. 144)

This is the critical moment of moral decision for David's father who chooses justice over loyalty to his family. This decision ultimately leads to Frank's suicide,

23. "'David, I believe that in this world people must pay for their crimes. It doesn't matter who you are or who your relations are; if you do wrong, you pay. I believe that. I have to.'" (Chapter 3, p. 150)

David's father is teaching his son a lesson that he never learned from his own father. In many ways, David's father's growth during this time of crisis has finally made Wesley a responsible adult, one who makes his own decisions based on what he thinks is right. David's father is no longer a slave to Julian Hayden's wishes.

24. "I find history endlessly amusing, knowing, as I do, that the record of any human community might omit stories of sexual abuse, murder, suicide . . . Who knows—perhaps any region's most dramatic, most sensational stories were not played out in public view but were confined to small, private places. A doctor's office say. A white frame house on a quiet street." (Chapter 3, p. 164)

This is the grown-up David talking with forty years of perspective on the events that changed his life. It is also, clearly, the author's point of view about life and reality and how appearances are very often deceiving.

25. "Two strokes. I used to think, my interest in symbol and metaphor far surpassing my medical knowledge, that they died from keeping the secret about my uncle Frank. They held it in, the pressure built, like holding your breath, and something had to blow. In their case, the vessels in their brains. In my father's

case, it was not only the secret he held in but also his bitterness. Which eventually turned into his cancer." (Chapter 3, p. 165)

David may be right in doubting his medical expertise, but he articulates a deep truth about how human beings suffer inside and cause damage to our bodies. Thus, while the truth of Frank's crimes and the actions of those who covered them up were omitted from history, David imagines that a certain kind of justice resulted in physical suffering in the form of strokes and cancer.

ESSAY TOPICS

1. *Montana 1948* is considered a coming-of-age story. In what ways is David a child at the beginning of the story? In what ways is he an adult by the time of his Uncle's death?

2. David's father's beliefs and actions change dramatically. At what point does he decide to follow the law rather than remaining loyal to his family? What influences him to arrest and hold his brother?

3. What is the source of David's mother's sense of right and wrong? How do her beliefs and actions change? What makes her tell her husband to release Frank after she has been so insistent that he be punished for his crimes?

4. David considers his father's attitude towards Native Americans racist. At what point does David's father change his views on equal rights for Native American people? Is David's father permanently "cured" of his racism?

5. Len, the deputy sheriff, says that a lawman in the West must learn when to look and when to look away. What would have happened if David's father had ignored Marie's accusations and not pursued a case against his brother?

6. Give three examples of the use of guns and firearms as symbols of emotions in the novel. Explain how each use of a gun depicts a specific emotion for the character involved.

7. In what ways does the town of Bentrock, Montana, in 1948 resemble a place in the Wild West of a much earlier time? How are conflicts and problems dealt with? Is the town a civilized place to live?

8. The mature David at 52 years old believes that keeping secrets has led to the strokes that killed his grandfather and disabled Len and that his father's bitterness induced his fatal cancer. What is the relationship between stress and health? Do you agree or disagree with David's diagnoses?

9. The novel is very clear in its depiction of white people's racist attitudes towards Native Americans. In what ways does the novel also describe social prejudice against women?

10. Why did David choose to be a history teacher rather than follow in his father's footsteps as a lawyer? Did David make the right career choice?

Made in United States
North Haven, CT
27 May 2022

19591886R00022